Practical
Simple Thai

p^3

This is a P3 Book
First published in 2002

P3
Queen Street House
4 Queen Street
Bath BA1 1HE, UK

ISBN: 0-75258-539-8

Printed in China

NOTE

Cup measurements in this book are for American cups.
This book also uses imperial and metric measurements. Follow the same units
of measurement throughout; do not mix imperial and metric.
All spoon measurements are level: teaspoons are assumed to be 5 ml, and
tablespoons are assumed to be 15 ml. Unless otherwise stated,
milk is assumed to be whole milk, eggs and individual vegetables such as potatoes
are medium, and pepper is freshly ground black pepper.

The nutritional information provided for each recipe is per serving or per person.
Optional ingredients, variations, or serving suggestions have
not been included in the calculations. The times given for each recipe are an approximate
guide only because the preparation times may differ according to the techniques used by
different people and the cooking times may vary as a result of the type of oven used.

Recipes using raw or very lightly cooked eggs should be
avoided by infants, the elderly, pregnant women, convalescents,
and anyone suffering from an illness.

Contents

Introduction

Anyone who loves Thai food will appreciate that it is a unique cuisine, distinctly different from the cooking of the countries that border it, but with many culinary influences from far beyond its geographical frontiers. Thai cooking owes many of its characteristics to climate and culture, but a history of centuries of invasions and emigration has played a large part in shaping its cuisine. The roots of the Thai nation can be traced back to the first century, at the time of the Chinese Han Dynasty, when the T'ai tribes occupied parts of South China along valuable trade routes between the East and the West. Over the years, the T'ai had a close but often stormy relationship with the Chinese, and eventually began to emigrate south to the lands of what is now northern Thailand, bordering Burma and Cambodia, then sparsely occupied by Buddhist and Hindu communities.

In time, the T'ai established the independent Kingdom of Sukhothai (translated as "dawn of happiness"), which eventually became Siam. The ports of Siam were the entrance to an important trade route, and ships from all over Europe and Japan docked there, or sailed inland along the rivers, bringing foreign foods, teas, spices, silks, copper, and ceramics. In the 1500s, the Portuguese introduced the chile to South-East Asia. The plant took immediately to the region's soils and climates, and continues to thrive. Trade with Arab and Indian merchants was important, and many Muslims settled in Siam.

The Kingdom of Siam survived until 1939, when it became the constitutional Thai monarchy, and 21st-century Thailand still reflects much of her past centuries of mixed cultures. The Thai people are independent, proud, creative, and passionate. Their love of life is apparent in the way they take pleasure in entertaining and eating. To visitors they seem to eat all day long. The streets and waterways are lined with food vendors selling a huge variety of tasty snacks from their stalls, carts, bicycles, and boats.

Thai people love parties and celebrations, and during their many festivals, the colorful, often elaborate and carefully prepared festive foods show a respect for

custom and tradition. Visitors are entertained with an unending succession of trays of tasty snacks, platters of exotic

fruits, and Thai beer, or local whiskey. When a meal is served, all the dishes are presented together so the cook can enjoy the food along with the guests.

Thai people take pride in presenting food beautifully. They carve vegetables and fruit into elaborate shapes and use them as garnishes. Their intricate patterns and skilled artistry are an integral part of their culture, which exhibits a deep appreciation of beautiful things.

Everyday life in Thailand is closely tied to the seasons, marked by the harvesting of crops and the vagaries of the monsoon climate. The Thai people take food seriously, exercising great care in choosing the freshest of ingredients, and thoughtfully balancing delicate flavors and textures. Throughout Thailand, rice is the most important staple food, the center of every meal. And coconut, in its various forms, has an almost equal place. Cooks in every region are expert at making the most of any ingredient available locally, so the character of many classic Thai dishes will vary according to the region in which they are cooked.

Fundamentals of Thai cuisine

The essential ingredients you need to have in order to cook Thai food are listed below. Of these, the most important are coconut, lime, chile, rice, garlic, lemongrass, gingerroot, and cilantro. With these you can create many traditional Thai dishes. Although many recipes have long lists of ingredients, the cooking methods involved in making them are simple enough even for inexperienced cooks to follow.

Balance is the guiding principle of Thai cooking, and the five extremes of flavor—bitter, sour, hot, salt, and sweet—are carefully and skillfully balanced in every dish and over several courses. Each dish therefore contributes to the balance of the entire meal.

Basil: three varieties of sweet basil are used in Thai cooking, but the variety commonly sold in the West also works well. Asian food stores often sell the seeds for Thai basil, so you can grow your own.

Chiles: the many varieties of chile vary from very mild to fiery hot, so choose carefully. The small red or green bird-eye chiles are often used in Thai dishes. They are very hot, so if you prefer a mild heat you should remove the seeds. Red chiles are generally slightly sweeter and milder than the green ones. Larger chiles tend to be milder. Dried crushed chilies are used for seasoning.

Coconut milk: this is made from grated, pressed fresh coconut. It is sold very widely in cans and longlife packs, in powdered form, and in blocks as creamed coconut. Coconut cream is skimmed from the top, and is slightly thicker and richer.

Cilantro: this is a fresh herb with a pungent, citruslike flavor, which is widely used in savory dishes. It wilts quickly, and retains its freshness best if bought with a root attached. Alternatively, you can grow your own.

Galangal: this is a relative of ginger, with a milder, aromatic flavor. Galangal is available fresh or dried.

Garlic: the pungent cloves of this bulb are used abundantly in Thai cooking, whole, crushed, sliced, or chopped, in savory dishes and in curry pastes. Fresh garlic can be bought widely, and pickled garlic is a useful purchase because it makes an attractive garnish.

Ginger: fresh gingerroot is peeled, grated, chopped, or sliced for a warm, spicy flavor.

Kaffir lime leaves: these leaves have a distinctive lime scent and can be bought fresh, dried, and frozen from specialty stores.

Lemongrass: this is an aromatic tropical grass with a lemon scent that is similar to lemon balm. Strip off the fibrous outer leaves and finely slice or chop the insides, or bruise and use whole. Lemongrass can also be bought dried in powdered form.

Palm sugar: this is a rich, brown, unrefined sugar made from the coconut palm and sold in solid blocks. The best way to use it is to crush it with a mallet or a rolling pin. Dark brown sugar is a good substitute.

Rice vinegar: mirin, or sweet rice vinegar, is used as a savory flavoring. If it is unavailable, sherry or white wine vinegar can be used instead.

Soy sauce: dark and light soy sauce are used for seasoning. The light sauce is saltier than the dark and is used mainly in stir-fries and with light meats. Dark soy sauce adds a mature, rich flavor and color to braised and red meat dishes.

Tamarind paste: the pulp of the tamarind fruit is usually sold in blocks. It gives a sour/sweet flavor. Soak the pulp in hot water for about 30 minutes, press out the juice, and then discard the pulp and seeds.

Thai fish sauce: also called nam pla, this is used like salt for seasoning, and has a distinctive, intense aroma. It is made from salted fermented fish.

KEY	
🍃	Simplicity level 1–3 (1 easiest, 3 slightly harder)
🥜	Preparation time
🕐	Cooking time

Chilled Cilantro Soup

This soup brings together Thai flavors for a cool, refreshing appetizer. It highlights fresh cilantro, which is now very widely available.

NUTRITIONAL INFORMATION

Calories	79	Sugars	.........5g
Protein	.........3g	Fat	...........3g
Carbohydrate	...13g	Saturates	.....0.1g

🍽 10 mins   🕐 35–40 mins

SERVES 4

I N G R E D I E N T S

2 tsp olive oil

1 large onion, finely chopped

1 leek, thinly sliced

1 garlic clove, thinly sliced

4 cups water

1 zucchini, about 7 oz/200 g, peeled and chopped

4 tbsp white rice

2-inch/5-cm piece lemongrass

2 lime leaves

1 cup fresh cilantro leaves and soft stems

chili paste (optional)

salt and pepper

finely chopped red bell pepper and/or red chiles, to garnish

1 Heat the oil in a large pan over medium heat. Add the onion, leek, and garlic, cover, and cook for about 4–5 minutes, stirring frequently, until the onion is softened.

2 Add the water, zucchini, and rice with a large pinch of salt and some pepper. Add the lemongrass and lime leaves. Bring just to a boil, then reduce the heat to low. Cover and simmer for about 15–20 minutes, until the rice is soft and tender.

3 Add the cilantro leaves, pushing them down into the liquid. Continue cooking for 2–3 minutes, until they are wilted. Remove the lemongrass and lime leaves.

4 Let the soup cool slightly, then transfer to a blender or food processor and puree until smooth.

5 Scrape the soup into a large container. Season to taste with salt and pepper. Cover and refrigerate until cold.

6 Taste and adjust the seasoning. For a more spicy soup, stir in a little chili paste to taste. For a thinner soup, add a small amount of iced water. Ladle into chilled bowls and garnish with finely chopped red bell pepper and/or chiles.

Thai Fish Soup

This is also known as *Tom Yam Gung*. Asian supermarkets may sell tom yam sauce ready prepared in jars, sometimes labeled "Chiles in Oil."

NUTRITIONAL INFORMATION

Calories	230	Sugars 4g
Protein	........22g	Fat 12g
Carbohydrate	....9g	Saturates 1g

🥢 🥢

🧊 25 mins   🕐 20 mins

SERVES 4

I N G R E D I E N T S

2 cups light chicken bouillon

2 lime leaves, chopped

2-inch/5-cm piece lemongrass, chopped

3 tbsp lemon juice

3 tbsp Thai fish sauce

2 small, hot, green chiles, seeded and finely chopped

½ tsp sugar

8 small shiitake mushrooms or 8 straw mushrooms, halved

1 lb/450 g raw shrimp, peeled if necessary and deveined

scallions, to garnish

T O M   Y A M   S A U C E

4 tbsp vegetable oil

5 garlic cloves, finely chopped

1 large shallot, finely chopped

2 large, hot, dried red chiles, coarsely chopped

1 tbsp dried shrimp (optional)

1 tbsp Thai fish sauce

2 tsp sugar

1 First make the tom yam sauce. Heat the oil in a small pan and add the garlic. Cook for a few seconds, until the garlic just browns. Remove with a slotted spoon and set aside. Add the shallot to the same oil and cook until browned and crisp. Remove with a slotted spoon and set aside. Add the chiles and cook until they darken. Remove from the oil and drain on paper towels. Remove the pan from the stove and reserve the oil.

2 In a small food processor or spice grinder, grind the dried shrimp, if using, then add the reserved chiles, garlic, and shallots. Grind together to a smooth paste. Return the pan with the original oil to the stove, add the paste, and warm through over low heat. Add the fish sauce and sugar and mix together. Remove from the heat.

3 In a large pan, heat together the bouillon and 2 tablespoons of the tom yam sauce. Add the lime leaves, lemongrass, lemon juice, fish sauce, chiles, and sugar. Simmer for 2 minutes.

4 Add the mushrooms and shrimp and cook for an additional 2–3 minutes, until the shrimp are cooked. Ladle into warm soup bowls and serve immediately, garnished with scallions.

Chicken & Coconut Soup

Make this soup when you want a change from traditional chicken soup. It is nicely spiced and garnished with a generous quantity of cilantro leaves.

NUTRITIONAL INFORMATION

Calories	76	Sugars 2g
Protein	......13g	Fat 1g
Carbohydrate	....3g	Saturates 0.1g

15 mins   40–45 mins

SERVES 4

INGREDIENTS

5 cups chicken bouillon

7 oz/200 g skinless boneless chicken meat

1 chile, split lengthwise and seeded

3-inch/7.5-cm piece lemongrass, split lengthwise

3–4 lime leaves

1-inch/2.5-cm piece fresh gingerroot, peeled and sliced

½ cup coconut milk

6–8 scallions, sliced diagonally

¼ tsp chili paste, or to taste

salt

fresh cilantro leaves, to garnish

1 Put the bouillon in a pan with the chicken, chile, lemongrass, lime leaves, and ginger. Bring almost to a boil, reduce the heat, cover, and simmer for

20–25 minutes, or until the chicken is cooked through. Pierce the chicken with a knife to check it is cooked through.

2 Remove the chicken and strain the bouillon. When the chicken is cool, slice thinly or shred into bite-size pieces.

3 Return the bouillon to the pan and heat to simmering. Stir in the coconut milk and scallions. Add the chicken and

continue simmering for about 10 minutes, until the soup is heated through and the flavors have mingled.

4 Stir in the chili paste. Season to taste with salt and, if wished, add a little more chili paste.

5 Ladle the soup into warm bowls and float a few fresh cilantro leaves on top of the soup to serve.

COOK'S TIP

Once the bouillon is flavored and the chicken cooked, this soup is very quick to finish. If you wish, poach the chicken and strain the bouillon ahead of time. Store them in the refrigerator separately.

Thai-Style Caesar Salad

This simple salad uses fried rice paper wrappers as crispy croûtons. The Thai fish sauce gives the dressing an unusual flavor.

NUTRITIONAL INFORMATION

Calories 533   Sugars 7g
Protein . . . . .4g   Fat 43g
Carbohydrate . . .35g   Saturates 5g

10–15 mins   2–5 mins

SERVES 4

I N G R E D I E N T S

1 large head romaine lettuce, with outer
  leaves removed, or 2 hearts

vegetable oil, for deep-frying

4–6 large rice paper wrappers or
  4¼ oz/120 g rice paper flakes

small bunch of cilantro, leaves stripped
  from stems

D R E S S I N G

⅓ cup rice vinegar

2–3 tbsp Thai fish sauce

2 garlic cloves, coarsely chopped

1 tbsp sugar

1-inch/2.5-cm piece fresh gingerroot,
  peeled and coarsely chopped

½ cup sunflower oil

salt and pepper

1 Tear the lettuce leaves into bite-size pieces and put in a large salad bowl.

2 To make the salad dressing, put the rice vinegar, fish sauce, garlic, sugar, and ginger in a food processor and process for 15–30 seconds.

3 With the machine running, gradually pour in the sunflower oil, until a creamy liquid forms. Season with salt and pepper to taste, pour the dressing into a pitcher, and set aside.

4 Heat about 3 inches/7.5 cm of vegetable oil in a deep-fat fryer to 375°F/190°C.

5 Meanwhile, break the rice wrappers into bite-size pieces and dip each into a bowl of water to soften. Lay them on a clean dish cloth and pat completely dry.

6 Working in batches, add the rice paper pieces to the hot oil and cook for about 15 seconds, until crisp and golden. Using a slotted spoon, transfer to paper towels to drain.

7 Add the cilantro leaves to the lettuce and toss to mix. Add the fried rice paper "crisps" and drizzle over the dressing. Toss to coat the salad leaves and serve immediately.

Thai Seafood Salad

This delicious seafood salad, which includes mussels, shrimp, and squid with light green vegetables, is best served chilled.

NUTRITIONAL INFORMATION

Calories	310	Sugars	4g
Protein	30g	Fat	18g
Carbohydrate	7g	Saturates	3g

🄖 🄖

20 mins, plus chilling   10–15 mins

SERVES 4

INGREDIENTS

1 lb/450 g live mussels

8 raw jumbo shrimp

12 oz/350 g squid, cleaned and sliced widthwise into rings

4 oz/115 g cooked peeled shrimp

½ red onion, finely sliced

½ red bell pepper, seeded and finely sliced

1 cup bean sprouts

2 cups shredded bok choy

DRESSING

1 garlic clove, crushed

1 tsp grated fresh gingerroot

1 red chile, seeded and finely chopped

2 tbsp chopped fresh cilantro

1 tbsp lime juice

1 tsp finely grated lime rind

1 tbsp light soy sauce

5 tbsp sunflower or peanut oil

2 tsp sesame oil

4 tbsp cold water

salt and pepper

1 Scrub the mussel shells and remove any beards. Discard any that are open or broken. Place the rest in a pan with just the water that clings to the shells. Cook over high heat for 3–4 minutes, shaking occasionally, until all the mussels have opened. Discard any that remain closed. Strain, reserving the poaching liquid, and refresh the mussels under cold water. Drain and set aside.

2 Bring the reserved poaching liquid to a boil and add the shrimp. Simmer for 5 minutes. Add the squid and cook for 2 minutes. When both are cooked through, remove them, plunge into cold water, and drain. Reserve the liquid.

3 Remove the mussels from their shells and put into a bowl with the jumbo shrimp, squid, and cooked peeled shrimp. Refrigerate for 1 hour.

4 For the dressing, put all the ingredients, except the oils, into a blender and blend to a smooth paste. Add the oils, reserved poaching liquid, 4 tablespoons of cold water, and season. Blend again to combine.

5 Combine the onion, bell pepper, bean sprouts, and bok choy in a bowl and toss with 2–3 tablespoons of the dressing. Arrange the vegetables on a large serving plate or in a bowl. Toss the remaining dressing with the seafood, then add to the vegetables. Serve at once.

Egg Noodle & Turkey Salad

A good dish for summer eating, this is light and refreshing, and easy to cook. The turkey can be replaced with cooked chicken.

NUTRITIONAL INFORMATION

Calories 355	Sugars 6g	
Protein 22g	Fat 10g	
Carbohydrate ...46g	Saturates 2g	

15–20 mins   5 mins

SERVES 4

INGREDIENTS

8 oz/225 g dried egg noodles

2 tsp sesame oil

1 carrot

1 cup bean sprouts

½ cucumber

2 scallions, finely shredded

5½ oz/150 g cooked turkey breast meat, shredded into thin slivers

chopped peanuts and basil leaves, to garnish

DRESSING

5 tbsp coconut milk

3 tbsp lime juice

1 tbsp light soy sauce

2 tsp Thai fish sauce

1 tsp chili oil

1 tsp sugar

2 tbsp chopped cilantro

2 tbsp chopped sweet basil

1 Cook the noodles in boiling water for 4 minutes, or according to the package directions. Plunge them into a bowl of cold water to cool, then drain and toss them in sesame oil.

2 Use a vegetable peeler to shave off thin ribbons from the carrot. Blanch the ribbons and bean sprouts in boiling water for 30 seconds, then plunge them into cold water for 30 seconds. Drain well. Next, shave thin ribbons of cucumber with the peeler.

3 Toss the carrots, bean sprouts, cucumber, and scallions together with the turkey and noodles.

4 Place all of the dressing ingredients in a screw-top jar and shake well to combine them evenly.

5 Add the dressing to the noodle mixture and toss together. Pile onto a serving dish. Sprinkle with chopped peanuts and basil and serve cold.

Hot & Sour Noodles

This simple, fast-food dish is sold from street food stalls in Thailand, with many and varied additions of meat and vegetables.

NUTRITIONAL INFORMATION

Calories .... 337 Sugars 1g
Protein .... 10g Fat 11g
Carbohydrate ... 53g Saturates 1g

10 mins   10–15 mins

SERVES 4

INGREDIENTS

9 oz/250 g dried medium egg noodles

1 tbsp sesame oil

1 tbsp chili oil

1 garlic clove, crushed

2 scallions, finely chopped

⅔ cup button mushrooms, sliced

1 cup dried Chinese black mushrooms, soaked, drained, and sliced

2 tbsp lime juice

3 tbsp light soy sauce

1 tsp sugar

TO SERVE

shredded napa cabbage

2 tbsp shredded cilantro

2 tbsp chopped toasted peanuts

COOK'S TIP

Thai chili oil is very hot, so if you want a milder flavor, use vegetable oil for the initial cooking instead, then add a final dribble of chili oil just for seasoning.

1 Cook the noodles in a large pan of boiling water for about 3–4 minutes, or according to the directions on the package. Drain well and return to the pan, then toss the noodles with the sesame oil and set them aside.

2 Heat the chili oil in a large skillet or wok and quickly stir-fry the garlic, scallions, and button mushrooms, until they are softened but not browned.

3 Add the black mushrooms, lime juice, soy sauce, and sugar and continue stir-frying until the mixture boils. Add the noodles and toss to mix.

4 Serve the noodles spooned over napa cabbage, sprinkled with shredded cilantro and chopped peanuts.

Thai Potato Stir-Fry

This vegetable dish has a traditional sweet-and-sour Thai flavoring. Tender vegetables are stir-fried with spices and coconut milk.

NUTRITIONAL INFORMATION

Calories ....138 Sugars 5g
Protein ....2g Fat 6g
Carbohydrate ....1g Saturates 1g

15–20 mins   15 mins

SERVES 4

I N G R E D I E N T S

4 waxy potatoes, diced

2 tbsp vegetable oil

1 yellow bell pepper, diced

1 red bell pepper, diced

1 carrot, cut into short thin sticks

1 zucchini, cut into short thin sticks

2 garlic cloves, crushed

1 red chile, sliced

1 bunch scallions, halved lengthwise

½ cup coconut milk

1 tsp chopped lemongrass

2 tsp lime juice

finely grated zest of 1 lime

1 tbsp chopped fresh cilantro

1 Cook the diced potatoes in a pan of boiling water for 5 minutes. Drain the potatoes thoroughly.

2 Heat the oil in a wok or a large skillet and add the potatoes, bell peppers, carrot, zucchini, garlic, and chile. Stir-fry the vegetables for 2-3 minutes.

3 Stir the scallions, coconut milk, chopped lemongrass, and lime juice into the mixture, and stir-fry the vegetables for an additional 5 minutes.

4 Add the lime zest and cilantro and stir-fry for 1 minute. Serve right away, while the vegetables are still hot.

COOK'S TIP

Check that the potatoes are not overcooked in step 1, otherwise the potato pieces will disintegrate when they are stir-fried in the wok.

Spiced Cashew Curry

This unusual vegetarian dish is best served as a side dish with vegetables, and rice to soak up the juices.

NUTRITIONAL INFORMATION

Calories 455   Sugars 6g
Protein . . . . .13g   Fat 39g
Carbohydrate . . .16g   Saturates 11g

10–15 mins, plus soaking

25–30 mins

SERVES 4

INGREDIENTS

1½ cups unsalted cashews

1 tsp coriander seeds

1 tsp cumin seeds

2 cardamom pods, crushed

1 tbsp sunflower oil

1 onion, finely sliced

1 garlic clove, crushed

1 small green chile, seeded and chopped

1 cinnamon stick

½ tsp ground turmeric

4 tbsp coconut cream

1¼ cups hot vegetable bouillon

3 kaffir lime leaves, finely shredded

salt and pepper

freshly boiled jasmine rice, to serve

1 Soak the cashews, in cold water overnight. Drain thoroughly. Crush the coriander, cumin seeds, and cardamom pods with a pestle and mortar.

2 Heat the oil and stir-fry the onion and garlic for 2–3 minutes, until softened but not brown. Add the chile, crushed spices, cinnamon stick, and turmeric, and stir-fry for another minute.

3 Add the coconut cream and the bouillon to the pan. Bring to a boil, then add the cashews and lime leaves.

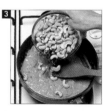

4 Season with salt and pepper. Cover the pan, lower the heat, and simmer for about 20 minutes. Serve hot, accompanied by jasmine rice.

COOK'S TIP

All spices give the best flavor when freshly crushed, but if you prefer, you can use ground spices instead of crushing them yourself in a pestle and mortar.

Thai-Style Crab Sandwich

A hearty open sandwich, topped with a classic flavor combination: crab with avocado and ginger. Perfect for a light summer lunch.

NUTRITIONAL INFORMATION

Calories	768	Sugars	........3g
Protein	........26g	Fat	.........49g
Carbohydrate	...58g	Saturates	.......8g

10 mins   0 mins

SERVES 2

INGREDIENTS

2 tbsp lime juice

¾-inch/2-cm piece fresh gingerroot, grated

¾-inch/2-cm piece lemongrass, finely chopped

5 tbsp mayonnaise

2 large slices crusty bread

1 ripe avocado

1 cup cooked crab meat

freshly ground black pepper

sprigs of fresh cilantro, to garnish

1 Mix half the lime juice with the ginger and lemongrass. Add the mayonnaise and mix well.

2 Spread 1 tablespoon of mayonnaise smoothly over each slice of bread.

3 Halve the avocado and remove the pit. Peel and thinly slice the flesh, then arrange the avocado on the slices of bread. Sprinkle the remaining lime juice liberally over the avocado.

4 Spoon the cooked crab meat over the avocado, then add any remaining lime juice. Spoon the remaining mayonnaise over the sandwiches, and season with freshly ground black pepper. Top with fresh sprigs of cilantro and serve the sandwiches immediately.

COOK'S TIP

To make lime and ginger mayonnaise, place 2 egg yolks, 1 tablespoon lime juice, and ½ teaspoon grated gingerroot in a blender. With the motor running, add 1¼ cups olive oil, drop by drop, until thick and smooth, and season.

Thai Green Fish Curry

This pale-green curry paste can be used as the basis for a range of Thai dishes. It is also delicious with chicken and beef.

NUTRITIONAL INFORMATION

Calories 217	Sugars 3g
Protein 12g	Fat 17g
Carbohydrate 5g	Saturates 10g

🥧 20 mins 🕑 15 mins

SERVES 4

INGREDIENTS

2 tbsp vegetable oil

1 garlic clove, chopped

1 small eggplant, diced

½ cup coconut cream

2 tbsp Thai fish sauce

1 tsp sugar

8 oz/225 g firm white fish, cut into pieces, such as cod, haddock, or halibut

½ cup fish bouillon

2 lime leaves, finely shredded

about 15 leaves Thai basil, if available, or ordinary basil

plain boiled rice or noodles, to serve

GREEN CURRY PASTE

5 green chiles, seeded and chopped

2 tsp chopped lemongrass

1 large shallot, chopped

2 garlic cloves, chopped

1 tsp freshly grated gingerroot, or galangal if available

2 cilantro roots, chopped

½ tsp ground coriander

¼ tsp ground cumin

1 kaffir lime leaf, finely chopped

1 tsp shrimp paste (optional)

½ tsp salt

1 To make the curry paste, put all the ingredients into a blender and blend to a paste, adding a little water if necessary. Alternatively, pound the ingredients together using a mortar and pestle. Set aside.

2 In a skillet or wok, heat the oil until almost smoking and add the garlic. Cook until golden. Add the curry paste and stir-fry for a few seconds. Add the eggplant and stir-fry for 4–5 minutes, until soft.

3 Add the coconut cream. Bring to a boil and stir until the coconut cream thickens and curdles slightly. Add the fish sauce and sugar and stir well.

4 Add the fish pieces and bouillon. Simmer for 3–4 minutes, stirring occasionally, until the fish is just tender. Add the lime leaves and basil, and cook for another minute. Remove from the skillet. Serve with plain boiled rice or noodles.

Lemongrass Chicken

An unusual recipe in which fresh lemongrass stems are used as skewers. The lemongrass imparts its delicate lemon flavor to the chicken.

NUTRITIONAL INFORMATION

Calories 140	Sugars 2g
Protein 19g	Fat 7g
Carbohydrate 2g	Saturates 1g

ⓖ ⓖ

🥙 25 mins   ⏱ 4–6 mins

SERVES 4

I N G R E D I E N T S

2 long or 4 short lemongrass stems

2 large boneless, skinless chicken breasts, about 14 oz/400 g in total

1 small egg white

1 carrot, finely grated

1 small red chile, seeded and chopped

2 tbsp chopped fresh garlic chives

2 tbsp chopped fresh cilantro

1 tbsp sunflower oil

salt and pepper

TO GARNISH

sprigs of cilantro

lime slices

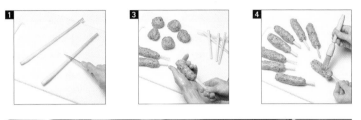

1   If the lemongrass stems are long, cut them in half across the middle to make 4 short lengths. Cut each stalk in half lengthwise so that you have 8 sticks.

2   Chop the chicken coarsely and place in a food processor with the egg white. Process to a smooth paste. Add the carrot, chile, chives, cilantro, and salt and pepper. Process for a few seconds to mix.

3   Chill the mixture in the refrigerator for 15 minutes. Divide into 8 equal portions. Use your hands to shape the mixture around the lemongrass skewers.

4   Brush the skewers with oil and broil under a preheated medium-hot broiler for 4–6 minutes, turning them occasionally, until golden brown and thoroughly cooked. Alternatively, barbecue over medium-hot coals.

5   Serve hot, garnished with sprigs of cilantro and slices of lime.

COOK'S TIP
If you can't find whole lemongrass stems, use wooden or bamboo skewers instead, and add ½ teaspoon ground lemongrass to the mixture with the other flavorings.

Rice Noodles with Chicken

The great thing about stir-fries is that you can use very little fat and still get lots of flavor, as in this light, healthy lunch dish.

NUTRITIONAL INFORMATION

Calories	329	Sugars	.........3g
Protein	........25g	Fat	..........4g
Carbohydrate	...46g	Saturates	.......1g

15 mins   10 mins

SERVES 4

INGREDIENTS

7 oz/200 g rice stick noodles

1 tbsp sunflower oil

1 garlic clove, finely chopped

¾-inch/2-cm piece fresh gingerroot, finely chopped

4 scallions, chopped

1 red bird-eye chile, seeded and sliced

2 cups finely chopped boneless, skinless chicken

2 chicken livers, finely chopped

1 celery stalk, thinly sliced

1 carrot, cut into short, thin sticks

5½ cups shredded napa cabbage

4 tbsp lime juice

2 tbsp Thai fish sauce

1 tbsp soy sauce

TO GARNISH

2 tbsp shredded fresh mint

slices of pickled garlic

sprigs of fresh mint

1 Soak the rice noodles in hot water for 15 minutes, or according to the package directions. Drain well.

2 Heat the oil in a wok or large skillet and stir-fry the garlic, ginger, scallions, and chile for about 1 minute. Stir in the chicken and chicken livers, then stir-fry over high heat for 2–3 minutes, until they begin to brown.

3 Stir in the celery and carrot and stir-fry for 2 minutes to soften. Add the napa cabbage, then stir in the lime juice, fish sauce, and soy sauce.

4 Add the noodles and stir to heat them through thoroughly, then sprinkle them with shredded mint and pickled garlic. Serve immediately, garnished with sprigs of fresh mint.

Crispy Duck with Noodles

A robustly flavored dish that makes a substantial entrée. Serve it with a refreshing cucumber salad or a light vegetable stir-fry.

NUTRITIONAL INFORMATION

Calories	433	Sugars	.........7g
Protein	........25g	Fat	..........10g
Carbohydrate	...59g	Saturates	.......2g

15 mins, plus 1 hr marinating   20–25 mins

SERVES 4

I N G R E D I E N T S

3 duck breasts, total weight about 14 oz/400 g

2 garlic cloves, crushed

1½ tsp chili paste

1 tbsp honey

3 tbsp dark soy sauce

½ tsp five-spice powder

9 oz/250 g rice stick noodles

1 tsp vegetable oil

1 tsp sesame oil

2 scallions, sliced

¾ cup snow peas

2 tbsp tamarind juice

sesame seeds, to garnish

1 Prick the duck breast skin all over with a fork and place the duck breasts in a deep dish.

2 Mix together the garlic, chili paste, honey, soy sauce, and five-spice powder, then pour it over the duck. Turn the breasts over to coat them evenly, then cover and put in the refrigerator to marinate for at least 1 hour.

3 Meanwhile, soak the rice noodles in hot water for 15 minutes. Drain well.

4 Drain the duck breast halves from the marinade and broil on a rack under high heat for about 10 minutes, turning them over occasionally, until they become a rich golden brown. Remove and slice the duck breasts thinly.

5 Heat the vegetable and sesame oils in a skillet and toss the scallions and snow peas in it for 2 minutes. Stir the reserved marinade and tamarind juice into the mixture, and bring to a boil.

6 Add the sliced duck and the noodles to the skillet and toss to heat them through thoroughly. Serve immediately, sprinkled with sesame seeds.

Stir-Fried Beef

A quick and easy stir-fry for any day of the week, this simple beef recipe is a good one-pan entrée. Serve with a simple green side salad.

NUTRITIONAL INFORMATION

Calories	583	Sugars	........13g
Protein	........40g	Fat	..........22g
Carbohydrate	...59g	Saturates	.......7g

10 mins   15–20 mins

SERVES 4

INGREDIENTS

1 bunch scallions

2 tbsp sunflower oil

1 garlic clove, crushed

1 tsp finely chopped fresh gingerroot

1 lb 2 oz/500 g tender beef, cut into thin strips

1 large red bell pepper, seeded and sliced

1 small red chile, seeded and chopped

3⅓ cups fresh bean sprouts

1 small lemongrass stem, finely chopped

2 tbsp smooth peanut butter

4 tbsp coconut milk

1 tbsp rice vinegar

1 tbsp soy sauce

1 tsp brown sugar

9 oz/250 g medium egg noodles

salt and pepper

1 Trim and thinly slice the scallions, setting aside some slices to use as a garnish.

2 Heat the oil in a skillet or wok over high heat. Add the scallions, garlic, and ginger and then stir-fry for 2–3 minutes to soften. Add the beef and continue stir-frying for 4–5 minutes, until browned evenly.

3 Add the bell pepper and stir-fry for an additional 3–4 minutes. Add the chile and bean sprouts and stir-fry for 2 minutes. Mix together the lemongrass, peanut butter, coconut milk, vinegar, soy sauce, and sugar, then stir this mixture into the wok.

4 Meanwhile, cook the egg noodles in boiling, lightly salted water for 4 minutes, or according to the package directions. Drain and stir into the skillet or wok, tossing to mix evenly.

5 Adjust seasoning with salt and pepper to taste. Sprinkle the beef and vegetables with the reserved scallions and serve hot.

Beef & Bell Peppers

A delicately flavored stir-fry infused with lemongrass and ginger. Bell peppers add color and it is all cooked within a few minutes.

NUTRITIONAL INFORMATION

Calories 230   Sugars 4g
Protein ....26g   Fat 12g
Carbohydrate ....6g   Saturates 3g

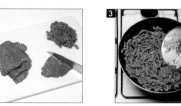

10–15 mins   10 mins

SERVES 4

INGREDIENTS

1 lb 2 oz/500 g lean beef tenderloin

2 tbsp vegetable oil

1 garlic clove, finely chopped

1-inch/2.5-cm piece gingerroot, finely chopped

1 lemongrass stem, finely shredded

1 red bell pepper, seeded and thickly sliced

1 green bell pepper, seeded and thickly sliced

1 onion, thickly sliced

2 tbsp lime juice

boiled noodles or rice, to serve

1 Cut the beef into long, thin strips, cutting across the grain.

2 Heat the oil in a large skillet or wok over high heat. Add the garlic and stir-fry for 1 minute.

3 Add the beef and stir-fry for an additional 2–3 minutes, until lightly colored. Stir in the lemongrass and ginger and remove the wok from the heat.

4 Remove the beef from the skillet or wok and keep to one side. Next add the red and green bell peppers and onion to the pan and then stir-fry over high heat for 2–3 minutes, until the onions are just turning golden brown and are softened slightly.

5 Return the beef to the wok, stir in the lime juice, and season to taste with salt and pepper. Serve with noodles or rice.

COOK'S TIP
When preparing lemongrass, take care to remove the outer layers, which can be tough and fibrous. Use only the center, tender part, which has the finest flavor.

Hot Beef & Coconut Curry

The heat of the chiles in this red-hot curry is balanced and softened by coconut milk, producing a creamy-textured and lavishly spiced dish.

NUTRITIONAL INFORMATION

Calories 230	Sugars 6g
Protein 29g	Fat 10g
Carbohydrate 8g	Saturates 3g

10–15 mins　　30–35 mins

SERVES 4

INGREDIENTS

1¾ cups coconut milk

2 tbsp Thai red curry paste

2 garlic cloves, crushed

1lb 2 oz/500 g braising steak

2 kaffir lime leaves, shredded

3 tbsp kaffir lime juice

2 tbsp Thai fish sauce

1 large red chile, seeded and sliced

½ tsp turmeric

½ tsp salt

2 tbsp chopped fresh basil

2 tbsp chopped fresh cilantro

shredded coconut, to garnish

boiled rice, to serve

1 Place the coconut milk in a pan and bring to a boil. Lower the heat and simmer for about 10 minutes, until the milk has thickened. Stir in the curry paste and garlic and simmer for an additional 5 minutes.

2 Cut the beef into ³/₄-inch/2-cm chunks, add to the pan and bring to a boil, stirring. Lower the heat and add the lime leaves, lime juice, fish sauce, chile, turmeric, and salt.

3 Cover the pan and continue simmering for 20–25 minutes, until the meat is tender, adding a little water if the sauce looks too dry.

4 Stir in the basil and cilantro. Sprinkle with coconut and serve with plain rice.

COOK'S TIP

Use a large, mild, red chile pepper—a fresno or a Dutch—because it will give the dish more color. If you use a Thai or bird-eye chile, you need only one because they are very hot.

Roasted Red Pork

This red-glazed, sweet, and tender pork dish is of Chinese origin, and makes a colorful addition to many stir-fries, salads, and soups.

NUTRITIONAL INFORMATION

Calories . . . . . . .276 Sugars 5g
Protein . . . . .34g Fat 13g
Carbohydrate . . . .7g Saturates 4g

10–15 mins, plus marinating   55–60 mins

SERVES 4

INGREDIENTS

1 lb 5 oz/600 g pork tenderloin

red chile flower, to garnish

napa cabbage, shredded, to serve

MARINADE

2 garlic cloves, crushed

1 tbsp grated fresh gingerroot

1 tbsp light soy sauce

1 tbsp Thai fish sauce

1 tbsp rice wine

1 tbsp Peking sauce

1 tbsp sesame oil

1 tbsp palm sugar or soft brown sugar

½ tsp five-spice powder

a few drops of red food coloring (optional)

1 Mix all the ingredients for the marinade together and spread over the pork, turning to coat evenly. Place in a large dish, cover, and put in the refrigerator to marinate overnight.

2 Place a rack in a roasting pan, then half-fill the pan with boiling water. Lift the pork from the marinade and place the meat on the rack. Reserve the marinade for later use.

3 Roast in a preheated oven at 425°F/220°C for about 20 minutes. Baste with the marinade, then lower the heat to 350°F/180°C and continue roasting for an additional 35–40 minutes, basting occasionally, until the pork is a reddish brown and thoroughly cooked.

4 Cut the pork into slices and serve on a bed of shredded napa cabbage, garnished with a red chile flower.

COOK'S TIP
The pork may also be broiled. Cut the meat into slices or strips and coat in the marinade, then arrange on a foil-lined broiler pan and broil under high heat, turning occasionally and basting with marinade.

Stir-Fried Pork with Pasta

This delicious dish, with its flavorful hint of Thai cuisine, will certainly get the taste buds tingling.

NUTRITIONAL INFORMATION

Calories 751   Sugars 10g
Protein . . . . .37g   Fat 27g
Carbohydrate . . .96g   Saturates 8g

20 mins   15 mins

SERVES 4

I N G R E D I E N T S

3 tbsp sesame oil

12 oz/350 g pork tenderloin

1 lb/450 g dried taglioni

1 tbsp olive oil

8 shallots, sliced

2 garlic cloves, finely chopped

1-inch/2.5-cm piece gingerroot, grated

1 fresh green chile, finely chopped

1 red bell pepper, cored and seeded

1 green bell pepper, cored and seeded

3 zucchini, thinly sliced

2 tbsp ground almonds

1 tsp ground cinnamon

1 tbsp oyster sauce

2¼ oz/60 g creamed coconut (see Cook's Tip, below), grated

salt and pepper

COOK'S TIP

Creamed coconut is available from Chinese and other Asian food stores and some large supermarkets. It is sold in the form of compressed blocks and adds a concentrated coconut flavor to the dish.

1 Heat the oil in a wok. Cut the pork into thin strips, season, and stir-fry for 5 minutes.

2 Bring a pan of lightly salted water to a boil. Add the taglioni and olive oil and cook for 12 minutes, until just tender. Set aside and keep warm.

3 Add the shallots, garlic, ginger, and chile to the wok and stir-fry for 2 minutes. Thinly slice the bell peppers and add to the pan with the zucchini. Stir-fry for 1 minute.

4 Finally, add the ground almonds, cinnamon, oyster sauce, and creamed coconut to the wok and stir-fry for 1 minute.

5 Drain the taglioni and transfer to a serving dish. Top with the stir-fry and serve immediately.

Thai-Spiced Sausages

These mildly spiced little sausages are ideal for a buffet meal. They can be made a day in advance and are equally good served hot or cold.

NUTRITIONAL INFORMATION

Calories 206	Sugars 0.1g
Protein 22g	Fat 11g
Carbohydrate 4g	Saturates 2g

20–25 mins   8–10 mins

SERVES 4

INGREDIENTS

14 oz/400 g lean ground pork

4 tbsp cooked rice

1 garlic clove, crushed

1 tsp Thai red curry paste

1 tsp ground black pepper

1 tsp ground coriander

½ tsp salt

3 tbsp lime juice

2 tbsp fresh cilantro, chopped

sausage casings (optional)

3 tbsp peanut oil

coconut sambal or soy sauce, to serve

1 Place the pork, rice, garlic, curry paste, pepper, coriander, salt, lime juice, and cilantro in a bowl and knead together with your hands to mix evenly.

2 Shape the mixture into 12 small link shapes. If you can buy sausage casings, fill the casings and twist at intervals to separate the sausages.

3 Heat the oil in a large skillet over medium heat. Add the sausages, in batches if necessary, and cook for about 8–10 minutes, turning occasionally, until they are evenly golden brown. Serve hot with a coconut sambal or soy sauce.

COOK'S TIP

These sausages can also be served as an appetizer—simply shape the mixture slightly smaller to make about 16 bite-size sausages. Serve with a soy dip.

Thai-Style Burgers

If your family likes to eat burgers, try these—they have a much more interesting flavor than conventional hamburgers.

NUTRITIONAL INFORMATION

Calories	358	Sugars 1g
Protein	. . . . .23g	Fat 29g
Carbohydrate	. . . .2g	Saturates 5g

20 mins

6–8 mins

SERVES 4

INGREDIENTS

1 small lemongrass stem

1 small red chile, seeded

2 garlic cloves, peeled

2 scallions

2½ cups closed-cup mushrooms

14 oz/400 g ground pork

1 tbsp Thai fish sauce

3 tbsp chopped fresh cilantro

sunflower oil, for cooking

2 tbsp mayonnaise

1 tbsp lime juice

salt and pepper

TO SERVE

4 sesame hamburger buns

shredded napa cabbage

COOK'S TIP

You can add a spoonful of your favorite relish to each burger or, alternatively, add a few pieces of crisp pickled vegetables for a change of texture.

1 Place the lemongrass, chile, garlic, and scallions in a food processor and process to a smooth paste. Add the mushrooms, and process until they are very finely chopped.

2 Add the ground pork, fish sauce, and cilantro. Season well with salt and pepper, then divide the mixture into 4 equal portions and use lightly floured hands to shape into flat burger shapes.

3 Heat the oil in a skillet over medium heat. Add the burgers and cook for 6–8 minutes, or until cooked to your taste.

4 Meanwhile, mix the mayonnaise with the lime juice. Split the hamburger buns and spread the lime-flavored mayonnaise on the cut surfaces. Add some shredded napa cabbage, top with a burger, and sandwich together. Serve immediately, while still hot.

Pork with Sesame Seeds

Thai cooks are fond of adding sweet flavors to meat, as in this unusual pork dish, with soy and garlic to balance the sweetness of the honey.

NUTRITIONAL INFORMATION

Calories 322	Sugars 8g
Protein 35g	Fat 14g
Carbohydrate ...13g	Saturates 4g

🥧 15 mins   🕐 40–45 mins

SERVES 4

INGREDIENTS

2 pieces of pork tenderloin, about
9½ oz/275 g each

2 tbsp dark soy sauce

2 tbsp clear honey

2 garlic cloves, crushed

1 tbsp sesame seeds

1 onion, thinly sliced into rings

1 tbsp seasoned all-purpose flour

sunflower oil, to cook

crisp salad, to serve

1 Trim the fat off the pieces of pork tenderloin and place them in a wide, nonmetallic dish.

2 Mix together the soy sauce, clear honey, and garlic. Spread this mixture over the pork, turning the meat to coat it evenly.

3 Lift the pork into a roasting pan or shallow, ovenproof dish. Sprinkle evenly with the sesame seeds.

4 Roast the pork in an oven preheated to 400°F/200°C for about 20 minutes, spooning over any juices. Cover the pork loosely with foil to prevent overbrowning, then roast for an additional 10–15 minutes, until the meat is thoroughly cooked.

5 Meanwhile, dip the onion slices in the flour and shake off the excess. Heat the oil and cook the onion rings, until golden and crisp, turning occasionally. Cut the pork into slices and serve with the fried onions on a bed of crisp salad.

COOK'S TIP

This pork is also excellent served cold, and it's a good choice for picnics, especially served with a spicy sambal or chili relish.

Jasmine Rice with Lemon

Jasmine rice has a delicate scent and it can be served completely plain, with no other flavorings. This simple dish has a light tang of lemon.

NUTRITIONAL INFORMATION

Calories . . . . . . .384 Sugars 0g
Protein . . . . .7g Fat 4g
Carbohydrate . . .86g Saturates 1g

5 mins   20–25 mins

SERVES 4

I N G R E D I E N T S

2 cups jasmine rice

3½ cups water

rind of ½ lemon, finely grated

2 tbsp chopped fresh sweet basil

1 Wash the rice in several changes of cold water, until the water runs clear. Bring 3½ cups of water to a boil in a large pan, then add the rice.

2 Bring the water back to a rolling boil. Turn the heat to a low simmer, cover the pan, and simmer for about 12 minutes.

3 Remove the pan from the heat and let stand, covered, for about 10 minutes.

4 Fluff up the rice with a fork, then stir in the lemon rind. Serve scattered with chopped basil.

COOK'S TIP

It is important to leave the pan tightly covered while the rice cooks and steams inside so that the grains cook evenly and become fluffy and separate.

Coconut Rice with Pineapple

Cooking rice in coconut milk, as in this dish, makes it very satisfying and nutritious. This method is often used as a base for entrées.

NUTRITIONAL INFORMATION

Calories 278	Sugars 11g	
Protein 5g	Fat 7g	
Carbohydrate ...54g	Saturates 5g	

🍚 10 mins   🕐 20–25 mins

SERVES 4

I N G R E D I E N T S

1 cup long-grain rice

2¼ cups coconut milk

2 lemongrass stems

1 cup water

2 slices fresh pineapple, peeled and diced

2 tbsp toasted coconut shavings

chili sauce, to serve

1 Wash the rice in several changes of cold water, until the water runs clear. Place the rice in a large pan with the coconut milk.

2 Place the lemongrass on a firm counter and bruise it by hitting it firmly with a rolling pin or meat mallet. Add it to the pan.

3 Pour in the water and bring to a boil. Lower the heat, cover the pan tightly, and simmer gently for 15 minutes. Remove the pan from the heat and fluff up the rice with a fork.

4 Remove the lemongrass and stir in the pineapple. Scatter the toasted coconut over the top of the rice and serve with chili sauce.

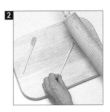

VARIATION

A sweet version of this dish can be made simply by omitting the lemongrass and stirring in palm sugar or superfine sugar to taste during cooking. Serve as a dessert, with extra pineapple slices.

Exotic Fruit Salad

This colorful, exotic salad is infused with the delicate flavors of jasmine tea and ginger. Ideally, it should be chilled for an hour before serving.

NUTRITIONAL INFORMATION

Calories	65	Sugars	........16g
Protein	.........1g	Fat	..........0g
Carbohydrate	...16g	Saturates	.......0g

15–20 mins, plus 1 hr chilling

0 mins

SERVES 6

INGREDIENTS

1 tsp jasmine tea

1 tsp grated fresh gingerroot

1 strip lime rind

½ cup boiling water

2 tbsp superfine sugar

1 papaya

1 mango

½ small pineapple

1 starfruit

2 passion fruit

1 tbsp lime juice

1 Place the tea, ginger, and lime rind in a heatproof pitcher and pour over the boiling water. Let stand to infuse for about 5 minutes, then strain the liquid.

2 Add the sugar to the liquid and stir well to dissolve. Let the syrup stand until it is completely cool.

3 Halve, seed, and peel the papaya. Halve the mango, remove the pit, and peel. Peel and remove the core from the pineapple. Cut the fruits into regular, bite-size pieces.

4 Slice the starfruit crosswise. Place all the prepared fruits in a wide serving bowl and pour over the cooled syrup. Cover the bowl with plastic wrap and chill for about 1 hour.

5 Cut the passion fruit in half, scoop out the flesh, and mix with the lime juice. Spoon over the salad and serve.

COOK'S TIP

Starfruit have little flavor when unripe and green, but when ripe and yellow they are sweet and fragrant. The tips of the ridges often turn brown, so run a vegetable peeler along each ridge before slicing.

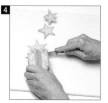

Lychee & Ginger Sherbet

A refreshing dessert after a rich meal, this sherbet is easy to make and can be served on its own or as a cooling side dish.

NUTRITIONAL INFORMATION

Calories 159	Sugars 40g	
Protein 2g	Fat 0g	
Carbohydrate . . .40g	Saturates 0g	

15–20 mins, plus freezing   0 mins

SERVES 4

INGREDIENTS

1 lb 12 oz/800 g canned lychees in syrup

rind of 1 lime, finely grated

2 tbsp lime juice

3 tbsp candied ginger syrup

2 egg whites

TO DECORATE

starfruit slices

slivers of candied ginger

1 Drain the lychees, reserving the syrup. Place them in a blender or food processor with the lime rind, lime juice, and candied ginger syrup and process until completely smooth. Transfer to a mixing bowl.

2 Mix the puree thoroughly with the reserved lychee syrup, then pour into a freezerproof container and freeze for 1–1½ hours, until slushy in texture.

3 Remove the sherbet from the freezer and whisk to break up the ice crystals. Whisk the egg whites in a clean, dry bowl until stiff, then quickly and lightly fold them into the iced mixture. Return to the freezer and freeze until firm. (To speed up this process in steps 2 and 3, you can use an ice-cream maker instead.)

4 Serve the sherbet in scoops, decorated with slices of starfruit and candied ginger.

COOK'S TIP

Do not serve raw egg whites to very young infants, pregnant women, the elderly, or anyone weakened by chronic illness. If you omit them from this recipe, freeze the sherbet again and whisk it a second time to ensure a light texture.

Bananas in Coconut Milk

The Thais like to combine fruits and vegetables, so it is not unusual to find mung beans or baby corn mixed with bananas or other fruits.

NUTRITIONAL INFORMATION

Calories	157	Sugars	........36g
Protein	.........2g	Fat	...........1g
Carbohydrate	...38g	Saturates	.......0g

10 mins   5 mins

SERVES 4

INGREDIENTS

4 large bananas

1½ cups coconut milk

2 tbsp superfine sugar

pinch of salt

½ tsp orange-flower water

1 tbsp shredded fresh mint

2 tbsp mung beans, cooked

sprigs of fresh mint, to decorate

COOK'S TIP

If you prefer, the mung beans could be replaced with toasted flaked almonds or hazelnuts.

1 Peel the bananas and cut them into short chunks. Place in a large pan with the coconut milk, sugar, and salt.

2 Heat gently until boiling and then continue to simmer for 1 minute. Remove from the heat.

3 Sprinkle over the orange-flower water, stir in the shredded mint, and spoon into a serving dish.

4 Place the mung beans in a heavy-bottomed skillet and place over high heat, shaking the pan occasionally, until turning crisp and golden. Remove the mung beans from the skillet and crush them lightly with a pestle and mortar.

5 Sprinkle the toasted mung beans over the bananas and serve the dish warm or cold decorated with a few sprigs of fresh green mint.